KU-444-281

Beer
Man's NEW Best Friend

Andy B & Jamien Bailey

BB

www.booksbyboxer.com

Published in the UK by
Books By Boxer, Leeds, LS13 4BS
© Books By Boxer 2014
All Rights Reserved

ISBN: 9781909732278

No Part of this publication may be reproduced or transmitted in any form
or by any means, electronic or mechanical, including photocopying,
recording or any information storage and retrieval system, or for the
source of ideas without written permission from the publisher.

Man and beer have been inseparable since ancient times. Remains of ancient ceramic beer pots, burned by the flames of ancient campfires have been found near ancient ceramic ring-pulls in ancient places such as Egypt where ancient red coloured lions used to roam. Many an ancient Egyptian after sitting round his ancient campfire and drinking from his ancient ceramic beer pot, has ended the night inside the Red Lion.

This book brings the story bang up to date and goes some way to explain the love affair between a man and his beer, giving some explanation to women who consider this to be an unhealthy relationship. The poor old dog, where often the man's dinner ends up in, that faithful non-critical friend who never complains, has to play second fiddle to the fickle blond who forever demands his masters affections.

Cheers!

I used to go walking the dog,

We'd both go out for a jog

But the dog's now the winner

As I'm getting thinner,

As my dinner ends up in the dog.

EX Best
Friend
🐾

The Friend That Will Always Beer There!

For as long as man has had the wherewithal (a big word not to be confused with "beer withdrawal") to ponder his own existence he has always nominated the humble dog as his one and only faithful companion - his true ally – his best friend.

You've got to admit, it's a nice thought. Dogs are cute and loyal and funny and some don't smell too bad but, over time, man has come to face the truth (you may want to cover the dog's ears if you're reading this aloud) - that man's true best friend is (and always has been) Beer!

Beer might not fetch a stick, lick your face or protect your house from intruders but at the same time, it won't leave you with a poohie carpet, chewed up furniture, bitten letters and 'biting' lawsuits, (unless you drink the really strong stuff!)

In this little book,
We take a little look,
At the love between a fella
And his Tetleys™, Guinness™ or Stella™

It's a bond that only man,
Can truly understand,
But women - don't you fear,

We love you too,

LET'S BE CLEAR...

THE
FIRST
ROUND

Yes, this first round is a serving of refreshing little insights into the fascinating world of men and beer. Beer makes men strong and intelligent. It allows them to carry out complicated tasks like adding up darts scores, flipping beer mats and working out whose round is next.

It gives them great insight into when a referee should visit his optician or if his parents were married when he was born. It also gives him the ability to spontaneously crack brilliant jokes, often very 'un PC' ones and generally within hearing distance of those who will be most offended.

But interestingly enough, these skills only seem to flourish within the confines of the male, beer drinking pack – a pack that you might refer to as The Brotherhood of Beer. For some reason, when a man blurts out some beer bolstered wisdom, or tells a lager lavished, hilarious joke to someone outside the confines of the cosy brotherhood then the magic doesn't seem to work.

This can result, at best, in deadly silence and at worst – a good thumping.

There's a very simple and obvious explanation for this… a lack of belief. Yes, like Santa Claus, beer skills only exist when you believe in them and whilst belief is strong within the Brotherhood – it is weak without. So the next time an outsider, a sober barmaid, for instance, informs you that the joke you told didn't make any sense, appeared to be a combination of two unrelated jokes with no punch line and was seriously flawed by continual burping – you can rest assured that it is purely down to a lack of belief on their part.

So, if you're already a member of The Brotherhood, get ready to re-familiarise yourself with our manifesto and for any non-believers who might be reading – prepare to be converted!

Beer is Born!

According to legend, the very first beer came from an ancient Sumerian (Iraqi), who left a loaf of bread out until the yeast fermented, giving him quite a buzz.

But don't try this at home. It is very difficult to drink bread and the green stuff mouldering round the edges will give you a nasty hangover. However it is a very cheap way of getting squiffy. Only try this if you.......knead the dough!

(And don't try that joke on anyone but your drunken mates!)

"Whenever the devil harasses you, seek the company of men or drink more, or joke and talk nonsense, or do some other merry thing. Sometimes we must drink more, sport, recreate ourselves, and even sin a little to spite the devil, so that we leave him no place for troubling our consciences with trifles. We are conquered if we try too conscientiously not to sin at all. So when the devil says to you: do not drink, answer him: I will drink, and right freely, just because you tell me not to."

Martin Luther

Two Drunken Monks

1st: "Drink is thine enemy"

2nd: "Love thine enemy"

We have a lot to thank religion for.

"For a Quart of Ale is a Dish for a King."
William Shakespeare

*"Milk is for babies. When you grow up
you have to drink beer."*
Arnold Schwarzenegger

*"Beer is my new religion,
and I am truly saved."*
Jamien Bailey

*"Beer makes you feel the way you
ought to feel without beer"*
Henry Lawson

*"Beer, the cause of and solution to,
all of life's problems."*
Homer Simpson

Before we go any further, it would be irresponsible of us not to remind you to always drink sensibly… that way you won't spill as much!

Brothers in Arms
(The King's Arms, that is)

We all like a beer with the lads,
And it really is one of those fads,
That no matter how old we become,
Never really stops being fun

We laugh and we jibe,
We stomp and we cheer…
Yes it's great to be alive,
With friends and with beer!

"Not all chemicals are bad. Without chemicals such as hydrogen and oxygen, for example, there would be no way to make water, a vital ingredient in beer."

Dave Barry

"As there is a pint of beer on the table , which is made up mostly of 2 parts hydrogen and 1 part oxygen, - do you think there's chemistry between us?"

Old drunk's chat up line

"I look like the kind of guy who always has a bottle of beer in his hand."

Charles Bronson

Game of Rounders Anyone?

It really should be easy,

to buy our drinks in rounds.

But things can get quite heated,

when memory dumbfounds!

Yes, it's the mathematical, scientific and sociological conundrum that baffles many a member of the Beer Brethren –
BUYING ROUNDS!

When drinking in a pair, on the whole, men are quite good at remembering whose round is next (but only quite good!). However, when numbers reach the dizzy heights of 3 or above – it can be a bit like watching a group of chimpanzees working through a Mensa™ puzzle – only not as dignified and with much more flatulence.

So What Are The Rules?

I suppose it depends on your own moral compass. If you know it's your round, you should, of course, speak up. However, if Robin Hood taught us anything – it was not only how to justify a devious act – but how to market it worldwide as an act of honour.
You could say he was the original spin doctor!

So, in the interests of playing devil's advocate, here's a Robin Hood style argument for deploying devious, round dodging tactics:

The situation is that you're invited out for drinks with some fellas who are considerably more well off than you. You fancy a beer so in all innocence, you accept. Then, as you walk into the trendiest bar in town and get a glimpse of the designer threads before being blinded by the bling on display, you feel a sudden pain in that most sensitive of areas – your wallet.

So, what do you do? Do you turn around and leave before your drinking buddies clock you? If you do this, you'll probably feel that you've let the lads down – that you have broken a golden rule of The Brotherhood. Plus, the wife's at home watching soaps. So, if you're going to stay, in that moment, you may have to commit to Robin Hood's Rule of Rounds – steal from the rich to give to the poor – aka – yourself!

Now, we're not recommending you steal anybody's wallet but if you're switched on – you can deploy a few tactics that will ease the strain on your modest, beer drinking budget. And here they are:

• Always be the first man out of the taxi and the last man at the bar.

• When rounds commence, try and negotiate it, so yours is the last in the sequence. This gives you the best chance of getting away with one.

• Strategically disappear when it's your round by going to the toilet, hanging your coat up or pretending to receive a mobile phone call. If you're stuck in a grid locked bar crowd, a quick duck to tie your shoe lace might suffice. (If people then notice you're wearing slip-ons however - you could be rumbled.)

• Take control. If you're the one to plan the group's route around the bars, you can make sure that you only ever visit cheap places (at least when it's on your round).

• Take advantage of memory loss. When the whole, 'who got the last round' conversation starts – claim it. Be ready, however, to plead confusion as your defence if the true buyer regains his memory!

• Play the victim and claim sympathy. This takes things to a new level but if your acting skills are up to it – you can pretend to have had your wallet stolen and solicit both sympathy and free drinks as you declare you will have to go home. A backfire can however result in you having to actually go home if sympathy doesn't stretch beyond a slap on the back and the arbitrary line "hard luck mate!"

• And finally; if you're morally bereft enough, you can borrow some cash from the person most drunk in your crowd. It's likely that they'll never remember lending you it!

But remember: Robin Hood never stole from the poor! At least, not in the Robin Hood Tavern!

So, when you're out with your real friends, financial peers or those with more financial cramp than yourself - the doctrines of The Brotherhood of Beer decree...

"Thou shalt not steal from thy brethren – no matter how skint thou art!"

Random Beer Trivia!

Did you know...
The first reference to beer dates to as early as 6,000 BC. The very first recipe for beer is found on a 4,000 year old Sumerian tablet containing the Hymn to Ninkasi, a prayer to the goddess of brewing.

And...
Prior to the invention of thermometers, brewers would dip their thumb or finger into the mix to

determine when the temperature was right for adding yeast. If it was too cold, the yeast wouldn't grow. If it was too hot, it would kill the yeast. It is thought that this practice gave birth to the phrase "rule of thumb."

The Rule of Thumb.

Like this!!

Alphabet Ale!

One of the few sentences in the English language to include every letter of the alphabet is:

Pack my box with five dozen liquor jugs

"Beer is proof that God loves us and wants us to be happy."
Benjamin Franklin

"If God had not intended us to drink beer, He would not have given us stomachs."
David Daye

"If wine was good enough for Jesus, beer is good enough for me."
Jamien Bailey

(more reasons to thank religion!)

"Beer makes people more lovable - but there are still some '8 pinters' around."
Ronnie Powers

"Drinking beer makes other people more interesting."
Alison Roper

"Drink provokes the desire but taketh away the performance."
Shakespeare

(+5 for beer!)

Mass Debate!

"They who drink beer will think beer."
Washington Irving

"He was a wise man who invented beer."
Plato

"I'm an old-fashioned guy... I want to be an old man with a beer belly sitting on a porch, looking at a lake or something."

Johnny Depp

"Paintings are like a beer, only beer tastes good and it's hard to stop drinking beer."

Billy Carter

"I don't think I've drunk enough beer to understand that."

Terry Pratchett, The Last Continent

"It's the beer talking!"

(Thank God! - I'm way too drunk to speak myself!)

"I am a firm believer in the people. If given the truth, they can be depended upon to meet any national crisis. The great point is to bring them the real facts, and beer."

Abraham Lincoln

To somebody outside 'The Brotherhood of Beer', a deep and meaningful conversation that arises after a beverage or two could possibly be construed as...

well... a load of old rubbish!

Men's conversations in the pub vacillate quickly between a multitude of subjects.

These can veer wildly from sex (the beddable merits of X Factor females, Big Brother contestants and the latest barmaid) to politics and war, to work, to films and video games, to the best pork pies and kebabs, who's gay (including most of the girls they've been rejected by.)

It continues as to the question of whether the Pope is circumcised, who's the best lover and who's round is it next.

Men don't discuss the emotional stuff
and indulge in gossip the way their female
counterparts do. They prefer instead to tell
stories, anecdotes, recall experiences, real,
imagined or made up. All stories are exaggerated.

Often no one listens to the raconteur
but watches his lips move, waiting for the
opportunity of a pause to launch in with their
own bit of wisdom.

Interruptions are not only allowed but
encouraged. Very little information is exchanged
or retained but all this makes for a jolly
atmosphere, which is what men's conversation is
all about.

But maybe, just maybe, beer is simply a lubricant
for the cogs of genius. It could be that at any
given moment in this big, wide world of 'Beer

Brethren', somewhere out there amongst the cogent calls of "down it" and "I've got the beer shits!" a beer brother, suitably oiled – is at this very moment untangling the meaning of life before the open mouths and eager eyes of his brethren. And, just as he is about to reveal the answer to this most ultimate of mysteries, a question is posed from the outer circle, that ever important and definitely worth interrupting for question…

…**"fancy a kebab?"**

Nobody puts Beer Belly in the corner!

Beer gives us not only the reason for life but for the rhythm of life. Shed of all inhibitions, we glide coolly onto the dance floor and perform the most complex gyratory body moves in front of attractive women who gape (in admiration we think) at this performance and we are amazed when they move rapidly away to the safety of their shrieking friends.

It's bad enough when we drink that we think we can dance, but what makes us think…

…it's better in underpants?

A Wee Trip to Jail?

We know it's hard to hold it in
once you've broken the seal,
But remember if you get caught short…

…*to keep your eyes well peeled!*

Be careful when you water the plants!

Random Beer Trivia!

Did you know…
The first consumer protection law ever written was enacted over beer by Duke Wilhelm IV of Bavaria in 1516. It was a purity law limiting the ingredients of beer to barley, hops and water.

And…
The powers that be at Guinness™ say that a pint of beer is lifted about ten times and each time about 0.56ml is lost in a beer drinker's facial hair. Maybe that's where the name 'beerd' comes from??

Indecent Proposal!

Be wary of mixing your vices,
Like gambling and women and booze
Coz if you don't quite have your eyes in…
you never know what you might lose?

The Munchies

"Never underestimate how much assistance, how much satisfaction, how much comfort, how much soul and transcendence there might be in a well-made taco and a cold bottle of beer."

Tom Robbins, Jitterbug Perfume

Drinking gives you the munchies,
And spicy food's a fave,
So when it comes to curries –
BEER = BRAVE!

balti bum burner

= The Perfect Combination

> *"Make sure that the beer – four pints a week – goes to the troops under fire before any of the parties in the rear get a drop."*

Winston Churchill
to his Secretary of War, 1944

> *"I have respect for beer."*

Russell Crowe

The Brotherhood of Beer -

The American Contingent

> *"You can't be a real country unless you have a beer and an airline - it helps if you have some kind of football team, or some nuclear weapons, but in the very least you need a beer"*

Frank Zappa

Random Beer Trivia!

Did you know…
The Pilgrims' plan was to sail further south in search of a warm climate but owing to a beer shortage, they landed at Plymouth Rock!

And…
The music for the American National Anthem, The Star Spangled Banner, was derived from a British drinking song called Anacreon.

So, since the forefathers fertilised American soil with good old British beer, our brothers across the pond have developed a proper relationship with this best of all friends (if you forget about the whole prohibition mishap!)

Not only did President Theodore Roosevelt take

over 500 gallons of beer with him on an African safari – the longest bar in the world is the 684 foot long New Bulldog in Rock Island, IL!

So, they really do know how to do it!
What's more, beer really was 'the taste to launch a thousand ships' in America as, believe it or not, the first United States Marine recruiting station was in a bar!

Beer and Sport!

"Depth perception and beer obviously weren't related."
Katie McGarry, Pushing the Limits

Remember the days when darts players were real men? In that they would saunter into the tournament and, after a warm up that included scratching their arses and burping, they would chug a pitcher of beer and throw some darts. Occasionally, some of them would hit the dartboard.

Well these days, bowling aside (which is less a sport in this country and more the kind of thing you do on your 12th birthday), there are very few sporting activities that you do well whilst drinking beer, including fighting, though some drinkers seem to ignore this.

So, as beer is our best friend, we tend to do what any best friend would do and make a compromise – we watch sport and we drink beer!

And as far as compromises go – it's not a bad one. As the footballers on the screen get more and more tense as the game goes on, beer helps us become more and more relaxed … until, of course, our team takes the game to penalties!

No amount of beer in the world could protect the male nervous system from the ravages of that particular eventuality.

"Life isn't all beer and skittles, but beer and skittles, or something better of the same sort, must form a good part of every British man's education."
Thomas Hughes

Pub Games!

Yes, as happy as man is with the avoidance of physical exercise whilst indulging in his favourite pastime of beer drinking, in the interests of getting a bit of the whole 'exercise thing' that people keep banging on about – pub games were invented. These are games that generally only require a level of dexterity akin to being able to fart and chew gum at the same time, and burn off the equivalent in calories of 1 pork scratching and a thimble full of beer.

They are however, great fun and favourites are:

- **Dominos** – apparently there's a strategy to this game but it's a secret closely guarded by the elderly so to everyone else, this is basically a game of luck.

- **Pool** – involves a lot of standing up but string a few lucky shots together in a game of 'Killer' and you could be quids in. Just try and make sure any winnings don't fall victim to 'wife tax'.

- **Darts** – not only does this game work the muscles in your throwing arm (which is usually an arm that has multipurposes for a man!) it also tests your mathematical skills. Definitely an educational element to this one.

Combine this game with beer and the old, motherly phrase of 'Careful, you could have someone's eye out with that!' , suddenly seems very appropriate. Not being able to see the numbers by over indulgence in beer does not appear to be a disadvantage to this game.

- **Table Football** – this is right at the top of the energy expenditure charts and promotes team work (which basically means a lot of shouting and blaming each other).
WARNING: Never challenge a German at this game – they are the best in the world so try and ignore those pangs of patriotism!

- **Coin Football** – there are probably a few variants of this but one of the most popular is the one where each player has three coins and takes it in turns to shoot at the opponent's goal (constructed using fingers on the edge of a table). As things get tense though, hands get moist and that's when mistakes can happen. Try and keep your hands dry at all times to reduce friction against the table. (and don't forget to pocket all the coins at the end!)

- **Skittles** – this is a bit old school but comebacks/money making re-marketing schemes use the term 'retro' all the time so if you find a pub that's either really behind the times, or on the cutting edge of retro fashion (telling the difference isn't necessary), then you might find yourself involved in a game of skittles. Skittles, we understand, is a kind of 'spit and sawdust' version of bowling. The aim is to try and make the pins fall down before you do.

• **Cards** – there are too many possible games to mention but it's hard not to associate card games in pubs with those bar room brawl scenes in old westerns. Poker is now back in many bars so maybe it's just a matter of time before there's a shoot out between card cheats at the Red Lion whilst the piano player plays on.

• **Tiddlywinks** – I struggled to spell the name of this game so I'll be damned if I'm going to look up the rules! If it's your thing – then go tiddlywink!

• **Board Games** – yes, many pubs have a stock of board games that you can borrow if you feel like exercising your brain. This means you can have a proper game of Cluedo™ – as opposed to that normal pub version that takes place when a mystery fart occurs – 'I think it was Dave, in the tap room, with the curry he had last night!'

• **Beer Mat Flipping** – when you actually make a correct 'flip', you look like Maverick in Top Gun. When you don't – you're more Turkey than Goose.

• **Darts** – Combine this game with beer and the old, motherly phrase of 'Careful, you could have someone's eye out with that!' , suddenly seems very appropriate. Not being able to see the numbers by over indulgence in beer does not appear to be a disadvantage to this game.

And finally...

• **Hide and Seek** – this is usually played when the wife comes to the pub to take you home.

ANOTHER ROUND?

Beer and Women!

Yes, this second round brings to the table some new and interesting characters that men like to call Women Folk.

Back in the day if you're were of the female variety, you would ask your man to order you a half of lager and lime (you weren't allowed to go to the bar yourself), sit in the snug (you were barred from the bar and the tap room) and don't speak until you are spoken to.

Women of course nowadays are the dominant customer base for most pubs often prefering pints or an expensive and sophisticated drop of Sauvignon, usually accompanied by a branded sparkly water. Women's 'spend' is often twice that of a man in a bar where it used to be merely a 'half'.

Beer and Women Trivia (marriage)

Did you know…

19th Century Englishmen who were about to tie the knot would take their mates out the day before the wedding for a final 'Bride Ale' – thus giving birth to modern, wedding related word 'Bridal'.

And…

It was the accepted practice in Babylon 4,000 years ago that for a month after a wedding, the father of the bride would supply his son-in law with all the mead he could drink. Mead is a honey beer, and because their calendar was lunar based, this period was called the 'honey month', or what we now know today as the 'honeymoon'.

Did you know…

A 'toast' (as in toasting the bride) comes from the custom of clinking glasses together. This was done vigorously in the bad old days so that some of the contents of each glass spilt into the other which would reduce the risk of being poisoned by the 'proposer of the toast'.

And…

The expression "got him over a barrel" has nothing to do with getting married. It refers to someone who is about to receive punishment. (Well, maybe it **does** have something to do with marriage!)

Beer and Women

"I've only been in love with a beer bottle and a mirror"

Sid Vicious

"Give me a woman who loves beer and I will conquer the world."

Kaiser Wilhelm

> *"A woman is a lot like beer. They smell good, they look good, and you'd step over your own mother to get one."*
> **Homer Simpson**

Women on Beer

> *"Give my people plenty of beer, good beer, and cheap beer, and you will have no revolution among them."*
> **Queen Victoria**

> *"I'm a meat girl and I just love having a beer."*
> **Jill Goodacre**

> *"Across the troubled maelstrom of time, people always need a beer."*
> **Ellen Kushner, The Fall of the Kings**

Beer vs Women

No hair pulling or scratching please!

Yes, if there's one rival for man's affection outside the wonderful world of beer; a component in his life that will not (and should not) be ignored, an enigmatic entity that carries the same loving lure as beer, another intoxicant, with the ability to make us feel like a king one minute and a fool the next - this has to be, of course; woman.

Now, as any well inducted member of the beer brethren will know, these two formidable forces will quite often lock horns and that leaves poor old man stuck in the middle, not knowing which way to turn, "Should I go to the pub and enjoy myself or should I go shopping with my woman?" (which should be a no brainer for a man until a rich spread of 'guilt' is applied, thickly, from the female direction.)

Now, for any woman reading this, you may be

cursing the invention of a drink that competes for your man's attention (or not as the case may be!). But according to some sources, those of you that are bothered may actually only have yourselves to blame – or your ancestors at least. In medieval europe, brewing and baking went together and, because of those nasty old gender roles we used to adhere to, that meant women were the first european brewers! Furthermore, a woman's beer brewing prowess would often earn her the much coveted title of 'ale wife' – a name that conjures the concept of being married to a beer soaked barrel bellied ale cart, perhaps… ring any bells, ladies??

Well, let it not be said that this book has no educational merit as we are, my friends, about to embark on that most academic of activities…
a debate!

Oh, hold on a minute – I've just been informed that a debate requires arguments to be made from both viewpoints. Hmm, well that makes this 'debate' a little one sided, to be honest, as following is a list of reasons why men might consider beer to be better than women...

1. Beer makes you forget your mistakes.
   (as opposed to bringing them up in arguments)

2. Beer goes well with the football season.

3. You can enjoy beer at any point in the month.

4. Beer never has a headache.

5. Treat a beer properly and you're guaranteed a good head.

6. You can have more than one beer in a night and not feel guilty.

7. You can share beer with your friends.

8. Beer makes social occasions less awkward.

9. You can't catch anything but a buzz from a beer *(but always use protection – i.e. a clean glass!)*

10. Beer = no mother in law.

11. Beer looks the same in the morning *(but if you think it looks great – seek help!)*

12. Beer doesn't need much storage space.

13. Beer never changes its mind.

14. Beer doesn't tell you how to mow the lawn.

15. Beer doesn't mind watching Die Hard films.

16. Beer doesn't make you watch the Eastenders omnibus.

17. Beer doesn't tape over the football with The Only Way is Essex.

18. Beer never asks "Does my bottle look big in this label?"

19. Beer doesn't wear a bra.

20. Beer likes ALL of your friends.

21. Beer doesn't try on 20 labels before you can go out.

22. Beer doesn't need the central heating on in summer.

23. Beer never needs a shelf putting up.

24. Beer doesn't mind how quickly you finish.

25. When it's finished – beer moves on *(and on and on…and on – once you've broken the seal!)*

26. And following on from the last one – beer likes the toilet seat leaving up!

27. Beer gets the truth out of you in a fun way.

28. Beer exaggerates your good points.

29. Beer doesn't watch Loose Women.

30. Beer would have read this list to the end – instead of stopping halfway through and saying *"This is stupid and immature. When are you going to grow up?"*

Random Beer Trivia!
(plus a rant!)

Centuries ago in ye olde England, patrons of our fine pubs deployed a genius tactic for achieving something that all pub patrons dream of – getting served quickly.

(It's amazing how many pubs would rather not pay for an extra hour of a bartendender's relatively modest wage, to lose a few hundred pounds in lost bar sales).

However...

These wily, olde worlde boozers would drink from mugs that had a whistle baked into the rim, thus allowing them to summon the bartender with a quick toot. It has been proffered that this pottery based piece of pub patron practice led to the well-known phrase:

Wet Your Whistle!

The Seven Day Rule

And, importantly, beer understands the **seven day rule**.

This is the rule that all men understand and women do not. The rule that states: all faults, indiscretions, thoughtlessness, bad behaviour, words said when under the influence, forgetting of important events, being late, not being observant enough, not doing jobs on time, insulting people, not being nice, not knowing that you're in trouble because she hasn't spoken for days, watching too much sport, lusting after other women and, sin of all sins, drinking too much beer - **are forgiven, forgotten and wiped off the slate after 7 days,** (and not brought up year after year, forever and ever, Amen)

Anyway – you get the idea. Beer could be better than women but that doesn't mean men don't want women around.

Women contribute the many positive things to a man's life like nice smells, hugs when we're down, the famous woman's touch and a constant reminder that we are the inferior partner in the relationship!

So, bearing all of the above in mind, man has quite a job on his hands to keep the two loves in his life happy and content.

Some may say this is impossible but…
In the true male spirit of grit and defiance,
Here are some examples of men really trying…

Putting the 'Man' in a Manhattan

When a cocktail bar opens in town,
Tom's girlfriend can't wait to get down
'What cocktail d'you want?', the waiter insists
'Gimme a lager … and a packet of crisps!'

Good Things Happen to Good People!

"My hobby could be described as drinking the most amount of beers in the shortest amount of time from 3.00 PM Friday to midnight Sunday and raising money for charity"

Bill Roberts
Self-confessed beer expert and alcoholic.

Home Blew!

"Give a man a beer, waste an hour. Teach a man to brew, and waste a lifetime!"

Bill Owen

Remember that making beer
is a very skilled occupation,
So brewing your own takes time and effort…

…and a lot of concentration!

D.I.Y.

Drink It Yourself!

Tom's wife leaves him at the weekend to do some renovation.
But soon regrets telling him to…

…"use your imagination!"

What Goes on Tour ... Goes Online

There used to be a time
When your antics never
reached her,
But now it's all online,
Thanks to social media…

RANDOM BEER TRIVIA

In the 11th century, Arnold of Soissons, a bishop in the Benedictine St. Medard's Abbey in Soissons, France, began to brew beer. He encouraged the locals to drink beer instead of water for its health benefits (beer was healthier than water mainly because it was boiled and thus sterilized from pathogens). No wonder they made him a saint!

*"From man's sweat and God's love,
beer came into the world."*
Saint Arnold of Metz
The Patron Saint of Brewers

*"All men hear is blah, blah, blah, blah, SEX, blah,
blah, blah, FOOD, blah, blah, blah, BEER"*
Denis Leary

Beer or Sex?

There's Tetley's™, Guinness™, Strongbow™ and
Becks™,
But are any of these really better than sex?
Sex is always upon a man's brain, so they say,
But with beer a good head is the only foreplay!
But 'Why?' you may cry, 'Can't a man have both
things?'
To deny and decry the pleasure both brings,
There's one tiny little thing of which I can
think…
***That men become useless, the more that
they drink!***

Top of the Flops

Remember guys – if you drink so much that you
wind up in a stupor, you could encounter…

...the Brewer's Drooper!

Boozing With Confidence

It's true when sober, for some,
Chatting up women's no fun,

So taking some magical beer,
Can often make nerves disappear.

But remember that finest of lines,
Between 'fresh' and 'out of your mind',

because girls aren't really too fond,
of that trick that you do with your wand!

Love Sick

If you're thinking of boarding the Love Boat,
Be careful how much you drink,
As before you're even out of the docks...
...you could well and truly sink!

Random Beer Trivia

Did you know…
Prohibition in America began on 16th January 1920 and lasted 13 years, 10 months, 19 days, 17 hours, and 32.5 minutes.
(Wasn't there a depression in the middle of that?)

And unsurprisingly…
Franklin Delano Roosevelt (FDR) was elected in 1932 because of his promise to end prohibition. Prohibition was rescinded on 5th December 1933 at 3:32 p.m.

(Looks like Frankie really did say Relax!)

Imperial Wisdom?

In 1116 BC, Chinese imperial edict stated that heaven required people to drink beer.

ONE
MORE
ROUND!

The 'H' Word

"Homer no function beer well without."
Homer Simpson

A friendship is based on more than just the good times. A friendship is an open and honest acceptance that occasionally, when things get tough, there will be some bad times. Our friendship with beer is no different.

As much as we celebrate our best friend, we have to accept that the 'day after the night before', in the company of this most convivial of companions can leave us feeling not quite on top form – to say the least.

Some people never get them, some people get them pretty badly and some people see them as a good excuse for lazing around and pigging out. Yes - it's the big, the nasty, the all-consuming 'H' word that is…

...The Hangover!

For a long time, people have strived to find a cure for this self-inflicted condition yet here we are in this most modern of eras still toiling under the beer soaked cloud of next day nastiness.
BUT...if there's one thing that we will forever try and convince ourselves that it actually works – it's the big, greasy, meat, egg and beans feast that is…

...The Full Breakfast!

No matter how rough we are, the sizzling scent of bacon wafting in our nostrils seems to have that magical affect of waking our senses and, for a moment or two, makes our stomach stop and think *"Yeah, I could go for that."*
But alongside the full breakfast (English, Scottish,

Welsh, Irish, Australian, American, Swahili or wherever), let's not forget the ally of all allies in our first, sugar loaded step towards re-hydration. This is the good old mug of tea or coffee. Our daily dose of the dark stuff is a totally different experience when hungover, as opposed to the normal, boring, morning routine.

The Salvation of the Infusion

That first, quivering sip, delivered to our dry, tongue-stuck mouth by clumsy, shaking hands that are 'tattooed' in stamps from clubs that we are glad not to be able to remember, is like the nectar of the god's and re-invigorates the very core of our booze destroyed being.

And so, breakfast and brew successfully down (for now!), we brethren take our first step into a day that will ideally follow a recovery programme consisting of:

- reading the paper (and breaking wind)
- watching the football (and breaking wind)
- partaking in a cheeky dose of hair of the dog (and breaking wind)
- followed by a curry for tea (and breaking wind… with the now increased risk of a follow through).

In reality, however, the punishment for indulging with our best friend, beer, may have actually only just begun…

Morning after Mysteries

Of course, after a heavy night, we don't always wake up in our own bed. This isn't always down to feral fecundity (look it up!), but more often than not, it just means that our true best friend, Mr. Beer, has decided to take us to a new place for some new experiences…

Jst Wnt 2 tell U I'm Soz!

It's the morning after the party,
And there's no point to pretend
So between being sick and the farting,
You text who you might offend!

So, to be on the safe side, you text everyone in your contact list including the boss, the vicar and your mother-in-law – just in case.

So, whatever your opinion of beer, it's hard to deny that it plays a pretty prominent role in the life of many a man. So much so, that beer has earned itself the prestigious title of... **man's true best friend!**

And like any relationship, man and beer have their ups and downs. So on that note, we'll leave you with some thoughtful little anecdotes from beer brethren about their own relationships with the one and only...

BEER!

"I have a total irreverence for anything connected with society except that which makes the roads safer, the beer stronger, the food cheaper and the old men and old women warmer in the winter and happier in the summer."

Brendan Behan

"Beer, it's the best damn drink in the world."
Jack Nicholson

"Beer, - the reason I get up every day at the crack of noon."
W.C. Fields

"The University of Nebraska says that elderly people that drink beer or wine at least four times a week have the highest bone density. They need it - they're the ones falling down the most."
Jay Leno

"Rugby is great. The players don't wear helmets or padding; they just beat the living daylights out of each other and then go for a beer. I love that"

Joe Theismann

"Prohibition makes you want to cry into your beer and denies you the beer to cry into."

Don Marquis

"I'm more of a guy's girl. I like having a beer in a bar, and I don't bicker or sit down and do my nails"

Zoe Saldana

"The big compliment came from the beer drinkers who didn't know me. They wouldn't drink or move when I sang. If they had their glasses in mid-air, the glasses wouldn't come down."

Ethel Waters

"I do condition my hair with honey and beer. I smell like the bottom of a beer barrel for days afterwards, but it's very good for the hair."

Catherine Zeta-Jones

"In my opinion, most of the great men of the past were only there for the beer - the wealth, prestige and grandeur that went with the power was of less significance"

A. J. P. Taylor

"I didn't think I could go on stage and play unless I had a beer to loosen up. Well, if it had been only one beer to loosen up, I'd probably still be drinking today."

Joe Perry

"The most frustrating thing for musicians who want to play stuff from the new album is when everyone goes out to buy a beer."

Joe Elliott

Beer Rocks!

Rock 'n' Roll

"It's the only job where having a drink at work is regarded as a great thing to do."

Will Harrison

"Je bois donc je suis"
("I drink therefore I am")
Descartes (when he was pissed!)

"When I was broke, no one ever offered to buy me a beer. Now that I have quite a bit of money, everybody tries to buy me beers. Where were all these people back when I was in college and broke?"
Chris Moneymaker

"Some people wanted champagne and caviar when they should have had beer and hot dogs."
Dwight D. Eisenhower

"Had an awesome time. You tell me to show up and all I have to do is drink beer, play guitar all day and I can lift weights and you're going to pay me for this!"
Zakk Wylde

"What I like about playing America is you can be pretty sure you're not going to get hit with a full can of beer when you're singing and I really enjoy that!"

Joe Strummer

"People care about my personal life. But really I'm dorky! I drink beer and go to football games. And ya know, sit in my house in a t-shirt on the weekends and play with my dog!"

Sophia Bush

"We were sitting on the bus one day and there were 5 of us hanging out. There was only one beer left in the cooler and we actually all took a little cup and split it. That was a pathetic day in rock and roll when five grown men have to be sitting there sharing a beer"

Zakk Wylde

"I can't actually read interviews with 'thesps' now because they're almost always fantastically predictable, the men especially. Actors are forever stressing their ordinariness, their beer and football-loving commitments."

Peter York

"I've been going long enough to prove what I wanted to prove, to get the girl I wanted to get, to make the money I wanted to make, to drink all the beer I wanted to drink. I've played - not exactly everywhere, but I've played enough places."

Joe Perry

"If they put fluoride in the water, the beer in all the pubs round here will taste of toothpaste."

Anon.

"My voice? Yeah, well, I used to drink a lot of beer when I was a kid and I sounded like a drunk in a choir. I don't drink anymore."

Eric Burdon

"It's mostly Mars Bars™ and peanuts and cheese and you go to the fridge and there's Red Bull™ and beer. It's not like people are holding me down and pouring beer in my face."

Graham Coxon

*"First year at university is all about **cramming**. You cram in the most amount of beer in the free time you have available."*

Paul Charles

A Pint to Prove
By A. Beerdrinker

There's many a cautionary tale

Of the danger that lurks in ale

And whilst they may all have a point

There's nothing quite like a good pint

A pint is a lot like a friend

You catch up with, now and again

It may not be wise when you're down

But can celebrate when things turn around

It can lubricate social events

Which are otherwise awkwardly spent

It can help wet a new baby's head

 And be raised for those who have left

It can taste of the place it was made

And be a symbol of good honest trade

It can be born of the field or the trees

It can taste of whatever you please

It's historic, it's culture, it's art

It's been known to cause potent wind

It's the treat of the hard-working man

And can be halved for his better half's hand ;-)

It's the sin that the holy man breaks

'It's just one pint for God's sake!'

It's quintessentially British

But The Danes - they know how to brew it

It's roast beef Sundays, it's fish and it's chips

It's a day at the seaside and last minute trips,

It's the "Let's get a taxi and have a drink tonight"

It will hate you forever if you ever drink
and drive

It's a dying event though, that one special pint,

As we race for oblivion on Saturday nights

So let's take that demon out of the drink -

Let's have us a pint, let's talk and let's think.

BEER JOKE!

The Best Beer in the World?

After the Great Britain Beer Festival in London, all the brewery presidents decide to go out for a beer.

The guy from Corona™ sits down and says, 'Hey Senor, I would like the world's best beer; a Corona™.' The bartender dusts off a bottle from the shelf and uncaps it.

The guy from Budweiser™ says, 'I'd like the best beer in the world, give me The King of Beers; a Budweiser™.' The bartender hands him a bottle.

The guy from Coors™ says, 'I'd like the only beer made with Rocky Mountain spring water, give me a Coors™.' The Bartender obliges.

The guy from Guinness™ sits down and says, 'I'll have a Coke™, please.'

The other brewery presidents look over at him and ask, 'Why aren't you drinking a Guinness™?' and the Guinness™ president replies, 'Well, I figured as you fellas aren't drinking beer, neither would I."

"The beer in this establishment is like making love in a canoe...

...it's f**king close to water!"
W.C. Fields

"Whiskey's too tough, champagne costs too much, vodka puts my mouth in gear. I hope this refrain, will help me explain, as a matter of fact, I like beer."
Tom T. Hall

"Beer is not a good cocktail party drink, especially in a home where you don't know where the bathroom is."
Billy Carter

And we bet you didn't know that…
The patron saint of beer is King Gambrinus
(not to be confused with St. Arnold, who is the
patron saint of brewing).

And…
The world's oldest trademark is the Bass™
symbol (a red triangle), which was registered in
1876.

Throwing a Sickie

"Work is the curse of the drinking classes."
Oscar Wilde

Don't drink coffee at work with a hangover. It makes it difficult to sleep it off in the afternoon.

"It's better to work and get paid when you have a hangover than sit at home in pain and poverty"

Lawrence Manning

*"Beer helps people keep in touch,
often by way of calls from ex-lovers at
3 in the morning"*
Helen Maginnis

*"Beer is the Danish national drink, and the
Danish national weakness is another beer."*
Clementine Paddleford

DRINK BEER AND WAKE UP IN
STRANGE PLACES

WITH NEW FRIENDS,

STRANGE CUTS AND BRUISES,

MISSING CLOTHES AND NO MONEY,

EXCEPT FOR POCKETS FULL OF
CHANGE

Serve your time with beer – Earn your time on Broadway!

Many actors started out as bartenders: **Sandra Bullock, Bruce Willis, Tom Arnold, Chevy Chase, Kris Kristofferson** and **Bill Cosby** to name a few.

So, as you have seen, the relationship between a man and his true best friend is not always in perfect harmony.

The relationship may become strained but it is a brave and desperate man who will turn his back completely on his true best friend.

In God We Trust

In Vino Veritas

In Beer Friendship and Oblivion

The lights come up,

The night is over,

So is this book,

It's time to get sober...

*By the way, before you go –
settle up at the bar will you?*

*We've been drinking on
your tab all night!*

> *"Always remember that I have taken more out of alcohol than alcohol has taken out of me."*
> **Winston Churchill**